D1379241

Dedication
To Joy and her three children,
Kurtis, Cherelle, and Clinton . . .
waiting to be butterflies.

In memory of our four special great-grandpas:
Grandpa Welch, Grandpa Barber, Granjar, and Opa.

Designed by Michelle Petz
Cover and interior illustrations by Kevin McCain

This story has been adapted from a children's story that was first published by Karen Holford as "Grandpa and the Changing Butterfly" in the *Family Ministries Planbook,* Department of Family Ministries, General Conference of Seventh-day Adventists, Washington, D.C.

Additional copies of this book are available by calling toll free 1-800-765-6955 or visiting www.AdventistBookCenter.com.

Library of Congress Cataloging-in-Publication Data

Holford, Karen.
   I miss grandpa : a story to help your child understand death—and eternal life / Karen Holford.
     p. cm.
   ISBN: 0-8163-2030-6
    1. Death—Religious aspects—Christianity—Textbooks. 2. Future life—Seventh-day Adventists—Textbooks.
  3. Christian education—Textbooks for children—Seventh-day Adventist. 4. Christian education—Home training. I. Title.

BT825.H74 2004
236'.1—dc22
                                               2004044350

04 05 06 07 08 • 5 4 3 2 1

Stevie was excited. He loved going to Grandma and

Grandpa's house. His mom and dad were going away for the weekend,

so Stevie and Grandpa would have the whole farm to themselves.

Grandpa let Stevie feed the chickens and lambs

and ride on the tractor. On Sabbath Grandma and

Grandpa took him to their tiny little church. There

was only one other boy there about Stevie's age.

His name was Jason. The best part was a little old

lady who always had treats hiding in her big black

purse for any boy who could answer a Bible question.

6

For Sunday lunch, Grandma let Stevie make ice cream

the old-fashioned way, with her ancient ice-cream maker.

They made it with lots of ice and cream from the farm cows

and fruit from the freezer.

Grandpa had a nap on Sunday afternoon. "I guess this side

of heaven I'm still gonna need my beauty sleep!" he said

before he settled down. Stevie liked the way the sun shone

on Grandpa's shiny old, bald head and sparkled in his

silvery whiskers. Stevie let him rest, and he went to the

garden to see Grandma.

Soon Stevie found caterpillars in Grandma's garden,

creeping about and eating leaves. Grandma showed him

a caterpillar turning into a chrysalis, wrapping itself up

in sticky thread. Then they found another chrysalis all

finished, hanging on a celery leaf. Grandma brought out

a jar to put the chrysalis and some leaves in so Stevie could

take the chrysalis home. "The chrysalis will turn into

a butterfly in a few days," Grandma promised.

Stevie tried to understand how a caterpillar, a chrysalis, and a butterfly were the same creature. How could they be the same when they were all so different? The chrysalis looked like a dried-up old leaf. Stevie felt sure it was dead, but he didn't want to disappoint Grandma by telling her so.

When his mom and dad came to fetch him, Stevie was tired but

very happy. "Next time I'll take you swimming in the river!"

Grandpa yelled as they drove away, waving. Stevie fell asleep

in the car on the way home, holding the jar with his chrysalis

inside. He was dreaming of riding on his very own tractor.

Two days later Stevie watched with his mom as the

chrysalis began to wriggle and split. They took the celery

leaves out of the jar and set them in their garden. Then they

sat and watched for a long time while that ugly little brown

package opened and the butterfly wriggled and squirmed

and pulled its wet, crumpled wings out of it. The butterfly

sat still for a long time on the leaves, until its wings were

dry and could open up.

And then Stevie saw all the pretty colors in the wings. He watched

as the butterfly spread the wings out wide, and it flew into the sky

for the first time. Stevie thought it was like watching a miracle! He

imagined how much fun he could have as a butterfly. Much more

fun than creeping about like a caterpillar, and eating celery.

Stevie saved the dried-up chrysalis skin. It was ugly, but it was kind of interesting. He put it in his treasure box with an old bird's nest and his special stone collection.

A couple of weeks later, Stevie's dad got a phone call.

When he put the phone down Dad was crying real tears.

Stevie had never seen his father cry before. Dad sat in his

favorite big chair and sobbed and sobbed. Mom came over

and hugged him, and Stevie patted his back, because he

didn't know what else to do. After a little while Dad pulled

Stevie on his lap and put his arm around Mom, and they

all had a big hug together. Bit by bit Dad's sobbing became

quieter, and then he gently explained what had happened.

Grandpa had been driving the tractor out on the farm when

he had had a heart attack. Having a heart attack means that

the heart gets sick and doesn't work properly anymore.

Sometimes when people have a heart attack they can die.

Grandpa had died, right out there on the farm. Grandma

missed him when he didn't come in for supper, and that's

when she went to look for him.

Now Stevie cried and cried and cried. He loved Grandpa, and they'd had lots of fun together. He would miss him so much. Grandpa had promised to take him swimming in the river next time he visited, and now he couldn't do that. Grandpa had said he would teach him to drive the tractor when he was big enough, and now he wouldn't be able to do that either.

Most of all Stevie would miss Grandpa just because he was his friendly, huggy, happy old Grandpa. Stevie would miss the smell of his farm clothes and the tickle of his whiskery beard. He would miss the way the sun shone on Grandpa's shiny head.

That night as he got into bed, Stevie asked his mom what it was like to die. Mom thought a long while and then she said, "Well, Stevie, death is a difficult thing to understand and talk about. But it's a bit like this. On this earth, we are like the caterpillars you found. We can do lots of things, but not all the exciting things God wanted us to do. Since sin came into the world our bodies here don't last very long. Everyone gets ill and worn out and eventually dies. It is sad when people die, because we miss them lots and lots and it hurts inside. But for people who love Jesus, like your Grandpa, dying is not the end of the story.

"Next week we will go to Grandpa's funeral, and Grandpa will be buried in the ground. I suppose that is a bit like when the caterpillar turns into a chrysalis. The caterpillar sleeps and doesn't know what is happening. Death is something like when you are asleep, and you don't dream or know anything at all.

Beloved Grandfather

"But one day, when Jesus comes back, He will take all the dead,

chrysalis-sort-of-bodies, including Grandpa's, and wake them

all up, and change them into something totally new and

amazing, something far more wonderful than we can imagine!

We will be beautiful and strong and we'll be able to fly.

We'll never be sad or sick again, and we'll live forever.

"The caterpillar in the chrysalis had to wait a while before it could be changed into a butterfly. We don't know how long it will be before Jesus will come again. But we know that He will, and then Grandpa will be strong, and he'll probably get all his hair back again too! And I guess that one of the first things that Grandpa will want to do in heaven is to find you and take you swimming in a crystal-clear river, just like he promised when you last saw him!"

"So Grandpa will remember me, and I'll recognize him, even with lots of hair and whiskers?" Stevie asked.

"Yes, and he'll recognize you even if you are quite grown up! With our new bodies Jesus will also give us back our special memories. Although we'll have different sorts of bodies, we will still be just us."

"I want to remember Grandpa in a special way, Mom.

Can I make like a book or something, and put pictures

of me and him in there? Could you write out some stories

for me, of the things Grandpa and I did together? I want to

stick that bit of chrysalis in there as well, to remind me that

one day Grandpa won't be dead anymore, but he'll be able

to fly around, like that butterfly. And the best thing I want

to put in there is a picture I want to draw of me and him,

swimming together in that river in heaven!"

Stevie felt sad at Grandpa's funeral. It was sad to say goodbye. Stevie cried a lot. Even after that, when he thought of Grandpa, he sometimes cried a bit too. But when he felt sad he went to look at his special "Grandpa and Stevie" book. He touched the chrysalis and remembered the butterfly flying away so beautifully. Then he thought of swimming in that river in heaven with Grandpa, splashing and laughing, and soon the smile came back to his face again.

For Parents

HELPING A CHILD COPE WITH THE LOSS OF A LOVED ONE

Death can be bewildering and scary for any one of us, and especially for a child. As a parent you will be experiencing your own sadness and facing different challenges. It may be helpful for you to find other people who can comfort and support you at this time.

Everyone experiences a death in a different way, and children are no exception. The most important thing to do is to create the space for your child to talk so you can listen to what they are thinking, and you can choose how to respond. It is helpful to accept whatever your child says and ask simple, open-ended questions to give you a fuller understanding of their thoughts.

Here are some practical ideas that may be helpful for you to think about.

- Encourage your child to talk about his or her ideas about the death. Children can feel somehow responsible for causing a death, so it's important to help them to understand why the person died and reassure them that they didn't do anything to cause the death.

- If possible, let your child attend the funeral. Explain everything that will take place so that your child can understand what will happen and make the choice whether to attend or not. It may be helpful to give your child a special role to play at the funeral, such as flowers to lay on the casket, or a short poem to read. Let them choose what to do, and have the freedom not to do it if they change their mind at the last minute.

- You could have a book at the funeral in which people can write their special memories of the loved one. Another option is to give out slips of paper to people and collect them to place in a book of memories for family members to read. Friends, colleagues, and neighbors may have very different memories of the person, and you may discover some surprising new stories.

- Perhaps you could invite your child to come and find you when he or she feels especially sad. One family had a "comfort chair," an old, squishy armchair with a soft blanket. Whenever a child was sad, his mother wrapped him in the blanket, sat in the "comfort chair," and hugged him till he felt better again.

- Help your child to make a special collection of memories in a box or in a book. Collect photos, stories, and cards sent to and from the loved one, a list of presents exchanged, and any special items that represent the relationship and are meaningful to your child.

- Make a small booklet with enough pages to allow one page for each month of the year. Your child could draw pictures of memories shared at different times — the loved one's birthday, family traditions, sledding in January, a visit to the sea in July, making a rabbit hutch together in October.

- You may like to choose a day for remembering the special person each year. It could be on their birthday or the anniversary of their death. Choose activities to do that become a tradition each year. This may be as simple as laying flowers on the grave; eating their favorite meal; or having a brief memorial service with some favorite hymns and a prayer.

- You could plant a tree in memory of your loved one. Your child can choose the tree and help to dig the hole and plant the tree. Take a photo each year of your child next to the tree to see how they both grow.

- At special events, when it feels as if someone special is missing from the gathering because they have died, you could light a candle in their memory, leave an empty chair, or place flowers or their photograph in the empty place.

- Let your child choose something from the loved one's belongings that they can keep always to remind them of the special person. It could be an item of clothing, a tool, a picture, a piece of furniture, or a cup. Help them find a way to keep it safe.

- Tell your child stories about the life of the person who has died. Maybe you could even write a miniature biography for your child, to fill in the gaps in their memory and give them a fuller picture of the person's life and achievements.

- Some children may like to have a link with the person who died at the special events of their life. If you find a half-finished tapestry, keep it for a granddaughter to complete when she's older, or finish it yourself, and give it to her made up as a cushion. Perhaps you can save other things from the loved one's belongings to give to your child at different stages in their life, such as a book when they start school, an old diary when they reach their teens, old love letters, or an item of clothing to wear at their wedding, and so on. You could say, "I think your grandma would have liked to have given you this today, if she were here."

- Every child is unique, and every relationship is different. Don't be afraid to ask your child what they would like, and what they think should happen, and let them know that they can always talk with you about the person who has died and ask you questions. Keep talking and listening to your child, so that you're always ready to help him or her through the grief process.

— Karen Holford